D0801867

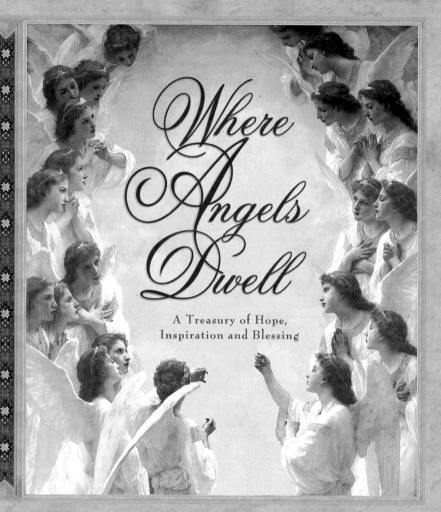

Where Angels Dwell

A Treasury of Hope, Inspiration and Blessing

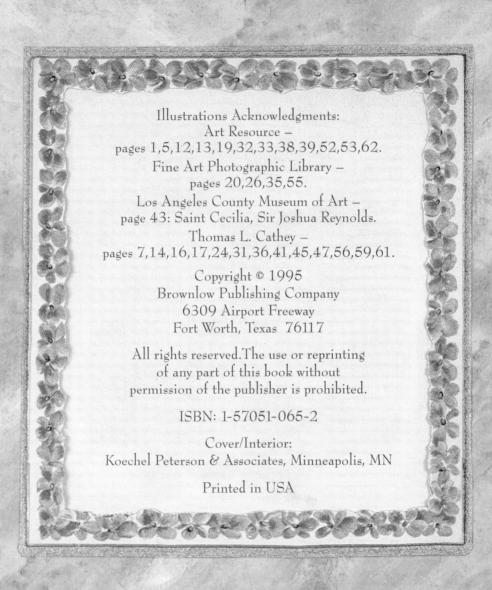

Illustrations Acknowledgments:
Art Resource —
pages 1,5,12,13,19,32,33,38,39,52,53,62.
Fine Art Photographic Library —
pages 20,26,35,55.
Los Angeles County Museum of Art —
page 43: Saint Cecilia, Sir Joshua Reynolds.
Thomas L. Cathey —
pages 7,14,16,17,24,31,36,41,45,47,56,59,61.

Copyright © 1995
Brownlow Publishing Company
6309 Airport Freeway
Fort Worth, Texas 76117

All rights reserved. The use or reprinting
of any part of this book without
permission of the publisher is prohibited.

ISBN: 1-57051-065-2

Cover/Interior:
Koechel Peterson & Associates, Minneapolis, MN

Printed in USA

A Special Gift

For:

_____

From:

_____

Date:

_____

Cherished Moments
Gift Books

A Basket of Friends

Merry Christmas With Love

Once Upon a Memory
Reflections of Childhood

Sweet Rose of Friendship

Tea for Two
Taking Time for Friends

Where Angels Dwell
A Treasury of Hope,
Inspiration and Blessing

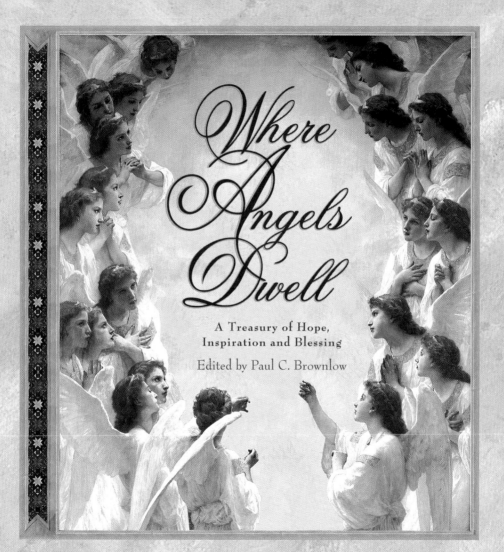

Where Angels Dwell

A Treasury of Hope, Inspiration and Blessing

Edited by Paul C. Brownlow

Angels Attend Thee

There are some spirits fitly strung
To echo back the tones of mine;

And those few, cherished souls among,
I dare, dear friends, to number thine.

Angels attend thee; may their wings
Fan every shadow from thy brow;

For only bright and loving things
Should wait on one so good as thou.

And when my prayers are pure and strong,
As they in my best hours can be,

Amid my loved and cherished throng,
I then will count, and pray for thee.

G. G.

Heavenly Friends

Let us not forget that the angels know each saint on earth more intimately than the saints themselves are known by their nearest friends. Just as earthly friends meet in later years, not as strangers but with feelings of intimacy and sympathy akin to those awakened by old kindred; even so will the saint, on reaching heaven, find God's angels to be, not strangers, but old friends who have known all about him from the day of his birth until the hour of his death.

NORMAN MACLEOD

Hearts on Fire

Then consecrate us, Lord, anew,

And fire our hearts with love;

That all we think, and all we do,

Within, without, be pure and true,

Rekindled from above.

FROM THE LATIN

Praise the Lord

Praise the LORD, you his angels,

you mighty ones who do his bidding,

who obey his word.

Praise the LORD, all his heavenly hosts,

you his servants who do his will.

PSALM 103:20, 21

The Angel of Patience

To weary hearts, to mourning homes,
God's meekest angel gently comes:
No power has he to banish pain,
Or give us back our lost again;
And yet in tenderest love, our dear
And Heavenly Father sends him here.

There's quiet in that angel's glance,
There's rest in his still countenance!
He mocks no grief with idle cheer,
Nor wounds with words the mourner's ear;
But ills and woes he may not cure
He kindly trains us to endure.

Angel of Patience! sent to calm
Our feverish brows with cooling palm;
To lay the storms of hope and fear,
And reconcile life's smile and tear;
The throbs of wounded pride to still,
And make our own our Father's will!

O thou who mournest on thy way,
With longings for the close of day;
He walks with thee, that angel kind,
And gently whispers, "Be resigned:
Bear up, bear on, the end shall tell
The dear Lord ordereth all things well!"

JOHN GREENLEAF WHITTIER

Hear the Angels Sing

Still through the cloven skies they come,
With peaceful wings unfurl'd;
And still their heavenly music floats
O'er all the weary world:
Above its sad and lowly plains
They bend on heavenly wing,
And ever o'er its Babel sounds
The blessed angels sing!

Yet with the woes of sin and strife,
The world has suffered long;
Beneath the angel-strain have rolled
Two thousand years of wrong;
And men at war with men hear not
The love-song which they bring:
Oh! hush the noise, ye men of strife,
And hear the angels sing!

E. Hamilton Sears

And I
have walked
with angels unawares
And upward mounted,
climbing over cares
A little nearer
to the Home
above.

GERALD MASSEY

If there
is anything
that keeps the
mind open to
angel visits, and
repels the ministry
to evil, it is a
pure human
love.

N. P. WILLIS

Tender Hearts

An angel's is a fine, tender, kind heart.
As if we could find a man who had a heart sweet all through,
and a gentle will; without subtlety, yet of sound reason;
at once wise and simple. He who has seen such a heart
has colours wherewith he may picture
to himself what an angel is.

Angels

Angels unseen attend the saints,

And bear them in their arms,

To cheer the spirit when it faints,

And guard the life from harms.

JOHN NEWTON

The Path of Life

The path of life we walk today

Is strange as that the Hebrews trod;

We need the shadowing rock as they—

We need, like them, the guides of God.

JOHN GREENLEAF WHITTIER

See, I am sending an angel ahead of you
to guard you along the way and to bring you
to the place I have prepared. Pay attention
to him and listen to what he says.

EXODUS 23:20, 21

Surely we are not told in Scripture about the angels
for nothing, but for practical purposes. For surely it is a
great comfort to know that wherever we go, we have
those about us who are ministering to all the
heirs of salvation, though we see them not.

S.J.C.

Love always provides for the object of its affection.
Just as loving parents make provision for the helpless babe,
even while it is unaware of the services rendered to it,
God's host have always been serving His elect.

ANDREW JUKES

Hallelujah

He feeds me, comforts, and defends,

And when I die His angel sends,

To bear me whither He is gone,

For of His own He loseth none;

Hallelujah.

No more to fear or grief I bow,

God and His angels love me now;

The joys prepared for me today

Drive fear and mourning far away;

Hallelujah.

J. HEERMANN

Our Noble Guardians

The angels are not only with you, but for you. They are with you to protect you, they are with you to help you. What should you render unto the Lord for all the benefits that He hath done unto you? For to Him alone be the honor and glory. Why to Him alone? Because it is He who orders it, from whom is every perfect gift. Nevertheless, although it is He who gives His angels charge over us, yet it is they who with such love obey His bidding, and nurture us in all our necessities. Let us therefore cultivate a generous and grateful spirit toward our noble guardians; let us love and honor them as much as we can and as is fitting.

BERNARD OF CLAIRVAUX

The

earth

is to

the sun

what

man

is to

the

angels.

Victor Hugo

Childlike Hearts

We pray for childlike hearts,

For gentle, holy love,

For strength to do Thy Will below

As angels do above.

Let me find in Thy employ

Peace that dearer is than joy;

Out of self to love be led

And to heaven acclimated,

Until all things sweet and good

Seem my natural habitude.

JOHN GREENLEAF WHITTIER

Nothing to Fear

They who on the Lord rely
Safely dwell though danger's nigh;
Lo! His sheltering wings are spread
O'er each faithful servant's head.
When they wake, or when they sleep,
Angel guards their vigils keep;
Death and danger may be near,
Faith and love have naught to fear.

HARRIET AUBER

Glad Searchers Sent

But angels on Thy face intent
With love we do not know—
Glad searchers of Thy will—are sent
To watch the way we go.

A. L. WARING

Could we forbear dispute and practice love, We should agree as angels do above.

EDMUND WALLER

The angel of the Lord encamps around those who fear him, and he delivers them.

PSALM 34:7

Spiritual Beings

Certainly there is nothing clearer or more striking in the Bible than the calm, familiar way with which from end to end it assumes the present existence of a world of spiritual beings always close to and acting on this world of flesh and blood. It does not belong to any one part of the Bible. From creation to judgment the spiritual beings are forever present. They act as truly in the drama as the men and women who, with their unmistakable humanity, walk the sacred stage in the successive scenes. There is nothing of hesitation about the Bible's treatment of the spiritual world. There is no reserve, no vagueness which would leave a chance for the whole system to be explained away into dreams and metaphors. The spiritual world with all its multitudinous existence is just as real as the crowded cities and the fragrant fields of Judea in which the writers of the sacred books were living.

PHILLIPS BROOKS

Glory on Their Wings

In solemn beauty, and in strength and power,
Comes the soul's guardian from his home afar,
To stand beside us in temptation's hour,
Pure as a glittering star.

They see all clear what mortals cannot know,
Each spring of thought the cloudless angels find;
Our dearest friends misjudge us, and are slow
Deciphering heart and mind.

They read our wants and give us tenderest care;
Tuned by one heart of love their bosoms beat;
They know the trials we are called to bear,
The thorns that pierce our feet.

They teach us mysteries of life and death
In the soul's silence breathing hallowed things
With heaven's hushed music in their fragrant breath,
God's glory on their wings.

E. BRINE

Listening Angels

Blue against the bluer heavens
Stood the mountain, calm and still.
Two white Angels, bending earthward,
Leant upon the hill.

Listening leant those silent Angels,
And I also longed to hear
What sweet strain of earthly music
Thus could charm their ear.

I heard the sound of many trumpets
In a warlike march draw nigh;
Solemnly a mighty army
Passed in order by.

But the clang had ceased; the echoes
Soon had faded from the hill;

While the Angels, calm and earnest
Leant and listened still.

Then I heard a fainter clamor,
Forge and wheel were clashing near,
And the Reapers in the meadow
Singing loud and clear.

When the sunset came in glory,
And the toil of day was o'er,
Still the Angels leant in silence,
Listening as before.

Then, as daylight slowly vanished,
And the evening mists grew dim,
Solemnly from distant voices
Rose a vesper hymn.

ADELAIDE A. PROCTER

The Imitation of Angels

We, who hope one day to partake of the nature of angels, should make it our delight even here below to imitate their heavenly tempers, and join in their holy employment; like them, to be ever ready to praise God and do His pleasure; to fulfill His commandments and hearken unto the voice of His words. As they tarry round about us to deliver us, and have charge over us to keep us in all our ways, so let us cherish and follow their holy influences. Thank God for them, and pray to Him to continue them to us. As they continually serve and praise God before His throne, so let us, their fellow-servants, strive to do His will on earth as they do it in heaven.

DEAN HOOK

For he will command his angels concerning you
to guard you in all your ways;
they will lift you up in their hands,
so that you will not strike your foot against a stone.

PSALM 91:11, 12

When Heaven in mercy gives thy prayers return,
And angels bring thee treasures from on high,
Shut fast the door, nor let the world discern,
And offer thee fond praise when God is nigh.

JOHN KEBLE

Arouse yourself; our Lord is speaking with you.
Do not wander off. His elect angels surround you,
do not be dismayed; the ranks of the demons
stand facing you, so do not grow lax.

EVAGRIUS

Honored Not at All

There have been ages of the world, in which men have thought too much of angels, and paid them excessive honor; honored them so excessively as to forget the supreme worship due to Almighty God. This is the sin of a dark age. But the sin of what is called an educated age, such as our own, is just the reverse; to account slightly of them, or not at all; to ascribe all we see around us, not to their agency, but to certain assumed laws of nature. This I say is likely to be our sin—the danger of resting in things seen and forgetting unseen things.

JOHN HENRY NEWMAN

When home is ruled according to God's Word, angels might be asked to stay with us, and they would not find themselves out of their element.

CHARLES HADDON SPURGEON

If heaven

is willing to sing to us,

it is little to ask that we

be ready to listen.

Nancy Gibbs

The Breath of Angels

It is sweet to feel we are encircled here,

By breath of angels as the stars by heaven;

And the soul's own relations, all divine,

As kind as even those of blood; and thus,

While friends and kin, like Saturn's double rings,

Cheer us along our orbit, we may feel

We are not lone in life, but that earth's part

Of heaven and all things.

P. J. BAILEY

A New Song

And now the prayer is turned to praise,
and with the angel-throng,
Who even now are pouring forth a new and joyful song,
Our hearts ascend, our whispers blend,
in deepest thrill of praise,
The happiest Alleluia hymn that human heart can raise.

FRANCES RIDLEY HAVERGAL

Not Alone

See, then, how great and holy we all are! You think no one cares for you, while apostles, patriarchs, prophets, martyrs care for you? They are leaning down, as it were, to watch you; they are a "cloud of witnesses" beholding you; they long for your company.

You think you are left alone and helpless, while the air is full of angels and heaven is full of prayers. How can you fret and grumble here, while you have such a home and such friends there who wait for you?

JOHN KEBLE

Ministering Angels

Angels of light, spread your bright wings and keep
Near me at morn:
Nor in the starry eve, nor midnight deep,
Leave me forlorn.

From all dark spirits of unholy power
Guard my weak heart,
Circle around me in each perilous hour,
And take my part.

From all foreboding thoughts and dangerous fears,
Keep me secure;
Teach me to hope, and through the bitterest tears
Still to endure.

If lonely in the road so fair and wide
My feet should stray,
Then through a rougher, safer pathway guide
Me day by day.

Should my heart faint at its unequal strife,
O still be near!
Shadow the perilous sweetness of this life
With holy fear.

Then leave me not alone in this bleak world,
Where'er I roam,
And at the end, with your bright wings unfurled,
O take me home!

ADELAIDE A. PROCTER

Springs of Devotion

There is a contemplative element in the service of the Seraphim—their activity is fed from the springs of their devotion. And so it must be with God's human servants. The activity which flows from ambition, the diligence which is purely mechanical and the result of habit, is not angelic diligence and activity. Our flying on God's errands will be an unhallowed flight, if we do not first secretly adore Him in our hearts. The ministry of angels, then, is only half their life. The other half, which indeed makes their ministry glow with zeal, is their worship.

DEAN GOULBURN

Thanks Be to Thee

Praise and thanks to Thee be sung,
Mighty God, in sweetest tone!
Lo! from every land and tongue
Nations gather round Thy throne,
Praising Thee, that Thou dost send,
Daily from Thy heaven above,
Angel-messengers of love,
Who Thy threaten'd Church defend,
Who can offer worthily,
Lord of angels, praise to Thee!

RIST

Angels are unsatisfiable in their longing to do by
all means all manner of good unto all the creatures,
especially the children of men.

RICHARD HOOKER

The Wings of Love

May the wings of Love enfold thee
Night and day;
May the strength of Love uphold thee
All life's way.

EUGENE S. FIELD

How angels gazed and wondered at the sight!
Had angels cause of wonder? Man has more;
Yes, dearest Lord, I wonder, love, adore!

ANNE STEELE

Kind words are the music of the world.
They have a power which seems to be
beyond natural causes, as though
they were some angel's song which
had lost its way and come to earth.

FREDERICK WILLIAM FABER

The Comfort of Their Care

I miss much comfort if I neglect what God
tells me of the holy ones whom He sends
to care for me. My Father gives me help and
cheer through human friends. So He uses
those strong pure beings who love to serve me
for His sake. He did not scorn their aid
in His own ordeal. I ought to be thankful for it.
Though I seem like Lazarus, cast out
and forgotten, I am in the thoughts of
God's good angels, who never tire of caring for me.

ANONYMOUS

In the house of God there is never-ending festival;
the angel choir makes eternal holiday;
the presence of God's face gives joy that never fails.

AUGUSTINE

Still I Would Serve

O the strangeness of the feeling!—
O the infinite revealing—To think how
God must love me to have made me so content!
Though I would have served him humbly,
and patiently, and dumbly,
Without any angel standing in
the pathway that I went.

DINAH MARIA MULOCK

Praise and glory be to God our Father forever and ever, Amen!